SEAGULLS REALLY CAN FLY

The Book

Sharon E. Jones Roberts

ISBN 979-8-218-87417-9

Majestic International Books
Chesapeake, VA

Majestic International Books.com

To Geneva Rivera – Thank you for giving me my first copy of *Jonathan Livingston Seagull*

For the Joshua Generations

For The Young

Although we organized these thought narratives only around biblical verses, we understand that the Bible is not the world's only source of wisdom and truth. The purpose of this book is to encourage, and to remind you of your innate goodness and divine ability. If you do not need encouragement, or if you do not identify with a religious tradition or that which we call God, we hope that you still can find something in these pages to inform or inspire you, as you make your life journey. For your peace, happiness and joy, we pray.

And when ye stand praying, forgive, if you have aught against any: that your Father also which is in heaven may forgive you your trespasses.

Mark 11:25

Forgiveness has been described as a process similar to peeling an onion- it is done in layers! When we come upon a new layer or aspect of our being where some resentment appears, there is more work to do. This does not mean our previous work with forgiveness was not effective. All effort is meaningful. We simply need to continue the forgiving process.

Sir John Templeton

Forgive

Don't let anyone make you hate them,
or anyone else, including yourself.
Live, love all.
Forgive, try to understand.
Never seek another's hurt to prove your
knowledge or your worth to yourself,
or to anyone else.
You - just as you are - you are beautiful.

And the Lord answered me, and said, write the vision, and make it plain upon tables, that he may run that readeth it. For the vision is yet for an appointed time, but in the end it shall speak, and not lie: though it tarry, wait for it; because it will surely come, it will not tarry.

Habakkuk 2:2-3

Write It Down

There's a maxim, plan or die. In business it means envisioning a goal and incorporating strategies and policies to attain it.
Your life is serious business. Your dream is a genuine goal; that goal is your present vision. You need to write it down!

In a notebook or planner, journal, computer or tablet, somewhere lay it out in print; think it out on in words.
Review and refine your plan as you grow; adopt habits that will help you to succeed.
Appreciate every victory. Push on despite any defeat.

Don't carry your life around in your head.
Think it.
Dream it.
Plan it and write it down.

And let us not be weary in well doing, for in due season we will reap, if we faint not.

Galatians 6:9

Persist

Some claim that when God is in something, it is easy to accomplish. So, if you experience difficulty, delay, or failure before the fulfillment of your quest, they contend that God is not in it; and at times you will be inclined to agree. Those are the times when you must persist.

The very nature of persistence is to press forward despite obstacles or opposition. Although there are some things that you will achieve without resistance, there are others that you will only achieve by perseverance and persistence.

Often people who gave up on their goals are the very ones who attempt to persuade others to forsake theirs. Consider that the next time someone ridicules you because of your goals or the problems you encounter as you toil to achieve them.

Rarely, do you find people who have fulfilled their dreams trying to convince someone else to abandon theirs. They realize, as most mockers likely do too, if you persist, the universe itself will insist that you receive what you believe in your heart, even know in your soul, you are destined to do, to have, and to be. Few things in life are easy or effortless. You must persist!

Study to show thyself approved unto God: a workman that needeth not to be ashamed; rightly dividing the word of truth.
II Timothy 2:15

"Are You Studying"

One of the best sermons I've heard was delivered by a thirteen year old at a youth service. She used the scripture, "Study to show thyself approved unto God...," as her text, and the question, "Are You Studying," as her subject. In her message, she spoke of her academic goals, what she thought she would need to do to achieve them, and young college graduates in her family from whom she drew inspiration. She delivered her message with the quiet eloquence of a thoughtful teenager, not the dynamism of the local pastor. Yet the power of her question, and her insightful union of scripture, subject, and narrative were as riveting as any ordained minister's homily.

Study is more than reading. It's also watching, listening, and reflecting. It is formulating your own questions and opinions about a topic, and correctly connecting new material with your prior knowledge and studies. On one hand, the purpose of studying is to learn; to acquire the basic information required to live. On the other hand, the purpose is to excel; to master some subject, including self, and the skills that will enhance the quality of one's life and service. Study is always a wise and beneficial use of your time.

Most conversations begin with some version of: hi, how are you or how have you been? What would happen if most of our conversations began with the simple question: hello, are you studying?

...commune with your own heart upon your bed and be still.

Psalms 4:4

Mediate upon these things, give thyself wholly to them; that thy profiting may appear to all.

I Timothy 4:15

Meditate

There are practices people use to enrich their religious and spiritual lives. Fasting, praying, meditation, and studying are the most well-known.

Fasting is abstaining from something, normally food, for a designated period. It usually is accompanied by prayer. Prayer, I was told, is the way people talk to God; meditation the way God talks to people. Study enhances understanding, in general, and in particular of the issues that are the focus of meditation and prayer.

If prayer, as the saying goes, is the key to heaven, meditation must be the key to God. Don't worry about sophisticated technicalities or techniques, just learn to be silent and sit still.

And there I will meet with thee, and I will commune with thee from above the mercy seat...

Exodus 25:22

Have a Private Meeting Place

A minister, who was the father of nine and the grandfather of many, once counseled his congregation, "always have a special place in your home where you go to be with God, even if it is only a chair."

It is instructive that all religious traditions have a place where their followers assemble for worship and prayer. Ordinary spaces become sacred places, even without elaborate architecture and imagery, simply because the space is a house of worship, a place of prayer.

This is also true for the individual. When you have a regular place where you go to pray, or sit to commune with God, that space assumes the atmosphere of prayer. In time, instead of you sitting in that place waiting on God, you find that as soon as you enter that room or sit in that chair, God is present waiting on you. Moreover, having a private meeting place will make you and that space a sanctuary - a dwelling place for the presence of God.

But they that wait upon the Lord shall renew their strength; they shall mount up with wings as eagles; they shall run, and not be weary; and they shall walk, and not faint.

Isaiah 40:31

But if we hope for that we see not, then do we with patience wait for it.

Romans 8:25

Waiting

Waiting can be difficult. Perhaps it's because God has given human beings so much power that we often think that we can snap our fingers, clap our hands, speak a word, and instantaneously command events, not only in own life, but also other people's, even the world.

Waiting is a reminder that human beings are subject to nature, and governed by God. There is an irrefutable and unavoidable wait factor in all of nature and in life. Seeds take to time to produce a harvest. Babies take months to be born. Goals take time to achieve.

Waiting is not the time for mindless idling, but mindful anticipation, proactive preparation. When you wait, wait with God for God. Wait fully confident in God's ability: the ableness and faithfulness that is uniquely God. Wait remembering that God works through human beings, including you, so labor while you wait. Wait understanding that God works with nature, never against it, although he is not confined by nature. God knows how to work the system: the laws of nature and life, to accomplish your expectation of Him, and His expectation of you.

Perhaps it's something unheard of, never seen or done before. So what! As one scripture so aptly states, "... men have not heard, nor perceived by the ear, neither hath the eye seen, O God besides thee, what he hath prepared for him that waiteth for him."

Hearken unto the voice of my cry, my King, and my God: for unto thee will I pray.

Psalm 5:2

And he spoke a parable unto them to this end, that men ought always to pray, and not to faint...

Luke 18:1

Keep Praying

It's possible to feel so oppressed by some aspect of life that you lose the discipline of prayer. It's not that you lose your faith. What you lose is the energy to exercise the practice of prayer; the energy, ironically, which regular prayer replenishes and provides. Simply put, you just don't feel like praying for some reason: unworthy, unhappy, unthankful, un – whatever it may be.

It's also possible to think you are just too busy to pray; too caught up in the euphoria of living to pause before you start your day, a moment or two throughout the day, or before you close your eyes at night, to speak a word of prayer. Again, you haven't lost your faith. You've lost the discipline of the practice of prayer.

It can't be insignificant, that despite different beliefs and customs, most of the world's religions encourage their adherents to pray periodically over the course of each day. Taking time to pray will allow you to re-focus, reconnect, and recharge yourself in a way that only humble, thankful communion with God can do.

Whatever your concept of God may be, and whatever the present circumstances of your life may be, keep praying. And when you pause to pray for yourself, always include a word of prayer for someone else.

Wisdom is the principal thing; therefore get wisdom: and in all thy getting get understanding.

Proverbs 4:7

The Education of Dr. Martin Luther King

Dr. Martin Luther King, Jr. believed that education was important, in general, and for the movement that he led. He told the journalist, Charleyne Hunter Gault, when she became one of the first two African Americans to attend the University of Georgia: "education is the key to our freedom."

As a truly educated person, Dr. King knew that education is more than formal schooling. Church and family were as important to his education as his formal learning. Dr. King's grandfather and father were ministers. His mother was a schoolteacher. He began school at age five. At that time, children were not allowed to begin school until age six. He said, "When his older sister started school, he thought he was smart enough to begin school too, and his mother agreed." Evidently, even at five, Dr. King was a talker, so when his teacher discovered that he was only five, he was required to leave school until the next year.

In the seventh grade, Dr. King's parents enrolled him in an experimental school sponsored by Atlanta University. The purpose of the school was to demonstrate that African American children could excel academically if given the same opportunity and advantages as white children were receiving. The year was 1941, fourteen years before the Supreme Court abolished segregation in public education in its landmark *Brown v. Board of Education* decision. The school closed after two years, but it made an enduring contribution to Dr. King's life. First, the curriculum, unlike that in most of the country at that time, included readings about

Harriet Tubman, Frederick Douglas, and other historic African Americans. Second, the academic quality of the school was so superior that Dr. King skipped the ninth and eleventh grades when he returned to the segregated public schools, and graduated from high school at fifteen.

After high school, Dr. King entered Morehouse College. His father also was a Morehouse man. Reverend Martin King, Sr. studied for twelve years to get his high school diploma and then graduated from Morehouse when he was thirty one. Initially, Dr. King planned to study medicine, but he quickly discovered that his love of words was greater than his love of science, so he decided to major in English and Sociology. As an English major, he was able to perfect his reading and writing skills. As a sociology major, he acquired understanding about the history and philosophy of human cultures and societies. In his senior year at Morehouse, Dr. King was ordained to the ministry and appointed the assistant pastor of Ebenezer Baptist in Atlanta, the church where his father was the Senior Pastor.

In 1948, Dr. King graduated from Morehouse and entered Crozier Theological Seminary in Chester, Pennsylvania. He was one of six African Americans in a class of one hundred. He graduated first in his class in 1951, and won a fellowship to continue his graduate work at the school of his choice. He selected Boston University, which he attended for four years. He spent two of those years studying philosophy at Harvard, and received his Ph.D. in Systematic Theology from Boston University in 1955.

When Dr. King completed the course work for his doctorate in 1954, he received several offers of employment. He was invited to pastor several churches, including northern churches, to join the faculty at three colleges, and to return to Atlanta to serve as the assistant pastor of Ebenezer Baptist. He elected to become the Senior Pastor of the Dexter Avenue Baptist church in Montgomery, Alabama. He was 25 years old. On December 1, 1955, when Rosa Parks refused to relinquish her bus seat to a white passenger, and the Montgomery Improvement Association subsequently organized the Montgomery bus boycott to protest segregation in public transportation, Dr. King was named the spokesperson for the protest, and the rest, as you well know, is history.

Dr. King's formal education merely gave him the language and the credentials to practice, preach, and teach the values and ideals that were instilled in him as a child. At Morehouse, he was impacted by Henry David Thoreau's essay on "*Civil Disobedience*" in which Thoreau explains his decision not to pay his property taxes as an act of social protest. At Crozier he studied the theologian Howard Thurman, and the activist Mahatma Gandhi. To some extent, he modeled his nonviolent protest on Gandhi's movement in India. These literary and historical persons, however, only mirrored Dr. King's childhood role models. His grandfather, Reverend Adam Williams, helped to lead a boycott against a local newspaper in connection with a protest for the establishment of a high school for African American students; the school where Dr. King subsequently attended. As a young child in Atlanta, he often saw his father refuse to comply with the demeaning requirements of segregation. Dr. King's life reflects the biblical principle: "train up a child in the way he should go, and when he is old, he will not depart from it."

Now if for any reason you suspect that your childhood training falls short of what you need to be your best self or realize your highest goals, don't despair. Just take the wisdom, the love, and the Spirit of God, and train, or if necessary, re-train and educate yourself.

... Therefore ye are my witnesses saith the Lord that I am God.
Isaiah 43:12

Don't Be Intimidated

Skeptics doubt that anyone can be anything other than ordinary. They expect the mundane, and are content with marginalization and mediocrity.

Haters get angry or jealous when anyone pursues the exceptional, or manifests the extraordinary. It makes no difference what the object of the pursuit, or the subject of the demonstration. They're the ones that if looks could kill...

Skeptics and haters want to make you feel inadequate, to cause you to shrink back from your work and the pursuit of your goal. They are trying, deliberately or unconsciously, to intimidate you. Don't let them!

Live your life, do your work, and pursue your goals with an intensity and a brilliance that even they will be compelled to concede, "Surely there must be a God somewhere."

For the Lord shall be thy confidence, and shall keep thy foot from being taken.

Proverbs 3:26

Cast not away therefore your confidence, which hath great recompense of reward.

Hebrews 10:35

Confidence

If you have a question, ask it. If there is something that you want to say, say it. If there is something that you want to do, that is right, do it! You shouldn't boast or be presumptuous, and may prefer to avoid self- promotion; but under no circumstances should you belittle or diminish who you are, what you think, or the good that God allows you to do and enjoy.

You owe no apology to anyone for living, for being exactly who life has made you. Yes, have faith in God, but also have faith in yourself. It's called confidence: a word of Latin origin which actually means with trust, or - with faith.

The Lord hath done great things for us, whereof we are glad.
Psalms 126:3

Finally, brethren, whatsoever things are honest, whatsoever things are just, whatsoever things are pure, whatsoever things are lovely, whatsoever things are of good report; if there be any virtue, and if there be any praise, think on these things.
Philippians 4:8

Smile

According to a very wise woman, people should always smile. She said, "it keeps the devil away!" In other words, a smile repels the negative thoughts and energy that would like to grasp you from within, or are directed toward you from without.

Think thoughts that fill you with gratitude and happiness, and even when you don't feel it, remember to wear your smile.

My tears have been my meat day and night, while they continually say unto me, where is thy God.

Psalms 42:3

Sometimes People Cry

Sometimes people cry because they're happy; relieved and amazed once again at an experience of the goodness and power of God.

Sometimes people cry because they're frustrated; baffled beyond endurance by the inability to do something, and the agony of the prospect that all their efforts toward that end were for naught.

Sometimes people cry because they're sad; possibly experiencing emotions that they are unable to verbalize: maybe they are angry; maybe they are grieving; they are hurting, and so they cry.

You shouldn't do it all the time, and you shouldn't do it for too long. But the truth is, sometimes people shed tears, then wash their face, and press on.

But the just shall live by his faith.
Habakkuk 2:4

Jesus said unto him, if thou canst believe, all things are possible to him that believeth.
Mark 9:23

When in Doubt

In the Bible, the terms faith and belief often are used interchangeably, but in life, faith and belief are not always identical. A belief is something that a person accepts as true. It is one level of awareness. In reality the belief may not be true, but for the person who believes it to be, it is; that is the nature and power of belief. A person's beliefs tend to change over time. Societal beliefs change as the collective knowledge of humanity expands. Toddlers often believe in the tooth fairy. Humanity once believed that the earth was flat.

Knowing is different from belief. It is another level of awareness. While beliefs are based on physical knowledge, information acquired via the physical senses, or mental reasoning, knowing can arises apart from any physical faculty. A person may believe something that is false, but one can only know what is true. It is possible to say we know of something that in truth we only believe.

Knowing also differs from faith. Although both knowing and belief can be the basis for faith. Faith, whether based upon belief or knowing, requires no physical evidence to validate it, that is the essence of faith, and what distinguishes it from belief. But like belief, faith that something is so, can make it so for that individual.

Everyone has faith in something. Everyone accepts as true something for which they have no physical evidence. Even the atheist has faith. Atheists accept as true that there is no reality called God. Though there is no irrefutable evidence that their conviction is true.

Babies are not born with beliefs, knowing, or faith. Children are taught their beliefs by the families, cultures, and societies in which they are raised. Obviously, there is value in growing up in a family, culture, or society that instills positive virtues and ideals, including faith in God.

While beliefs can be taught, faith: what you choose to believe without physical evidence, about the Divine, the universe, yourself and your abilities must be chosen. The choice of faith is not a onetime event, but a way of living. It must be nurtured. Even if you are graced to know, it is necessary to intentionally nurture your faith.

Notwithstanding belief, knowing, and faith, there may come a time when you begin to doubt some or all that you have been taught. An episode of doubt may occur as you make your thinking your own. But when you are confronted by doubt, remember what you know, and the best of what you believe, and firmly hold fast to faith.

Whoso keepeth his mouth and his tongue keepeth his soul from trouble.

Proverbs 21:23

On Questions

If you don't have an answer for a question, don't invent one. It's alright to say I don't know, I'd like to think about that, and if appropriate, I'll get back to you. Questions can be tricky. If you haven't anticipated the question, to answer it can be detrimental.

Then there are those questions that are not questions at all: the rhetorical; and the questions that are not asked to be answered, but to be pondered.

In any event, you should never yield to the pressure to answer a question for which you really have no answer. Under no circumstances should you fudge it, fake it, or force it. If you haven't considered what is being asked, just politely and gracefully decline to reply.

Someone may not like it, or think you less than for doing so, but there's a verse in Proverbs that says, "Even a fool, when he holdeth his peace is counted wise, and he that shutteth his lips is esteemed a man of understanding."

By humility and the fear of the Lord are riches, and honor, and life.

Proverbs 22:4

Stay Green

I have often heard this expression, "stay green." Generally it means stay humble, stay teachable, stay flexible. Although green can indicate immaturity or inexperience, it usually is associated with growth: someone who is not only alive, but also improving in their living from season to season and from year to year.

This expression reminds us of the mystery of the Divine. That it is never about compelling God to do our will, and always about conforming ourselves to His will. It is never about insisting that we have things our way. It is always about learning to yield ourselves to God's way.

One reason affluence and influence carry such responsibility is because people with economic might or in positions of power can, if they choose, force their way through life. They can have their own way in many situations, and impose their will on others by virtue of their wealth or authority.

It takes a lot of wisdom, understanding, and restraint to have the freedom and the resources to do whatever you want, and yet maintain the humility only to do what God directs.

Of course some will say that God is not the least bit concerned about the ordinary day to day affairs of your life. You will need to stay green to know that if you want Him to be, and permit Him to be, He is.

A new commandment I give unto you, that ye love one another; as I have loved you, that ye also love one another. By this shall all men know that ye are my disciples, if ye have love one to another.

John 13:34-35

Perfection

Walter Fluker, a college professor and theologian, conducted a comparative study of the idea of community in the thought of two revered twentieth century theologians, Howard Thurman and Martin Luther King, Jr.. Howard Thurman met with Mahatma Gandhi in 1935. Gandhi questioned whether Christianity could be the catalyst for a nonviolent resistance movement for social change similar to the one he led in India. Thurman was convinced that "true" Christianity should be the mechanism for generating racial equality and positive social change. When he returned to the United States, he traveled the country attempting to persuade his Christian community of his conviction, and wrote of it in a celebrated text, *Jesus and the Disinherited.* As a student, Martin Luther King, Jr. read Thurman's book, and as a civil rights leader is said to have kept a copy of it in his briefcase. Fluker, who personally knew Thurman and King concluded, unsurprisingly, that the key to both men's concept of community was love.

Fluker documented his findings in a lovely publication, *They Looked for a City.* The book is just one in an innumerable array of books, essays, sermons, speeches, poems, songs and reports, which unanimously proclaim that love is the universal unifier. In view of humanity's long held consensus about love, it is perplexing that all facets of the human community: family, school, religious institutions, neighborhood, city, county, state, country, and world have an immense love deficit.

In the American classic that partially inspired this project, *Jonathan Livingston Seagull,* Jonathan is admonished in his last conversation with his teacher, "Keep working on perfection Jon, keep working on love." Timeless wisdom! "Keep working on perfection," humanity, individually and collectively, "keep working on love."

Commit thy way unto the Lord; trust also in him; and he shall bring it to pass.

Psalm 37:5

Now unto him that is able to do exceeding abundantly above all that we ask or think, according to the power that worketh in us.

Ephesians 3:20

Trust God

Richard Bach's beautiful story, *Jonathan Livingston Seagull,* tells the classic tale of the mythical hero, the dreamer, the seeker, the explorer of life and self. The person with an intense yearning to do, to learn, to have, to become more than what is considered appropriate or acceptable in the community or environment of his birth. Inevitably, in response to this burning desire, the hero is compelled to leave the repression of the status quo; or as in the case of Jonathan Seagull, he is propelled by expulsion to leave the comfort and confinement of the flock and strike out in response to his burning desire to fly.

The pain of ejection is eased by the freedom he then enjoys to develop and express his yearning without restriction, or the fear of ridicule or repercussion. Inevitably, he encounters likeminded souls who share his desire to do, as well as his faith that it can be done. Thus he is no longer alone, but has the blessing of companionship, fellowship, and real camaraderie. Eventually, he meets his teacher, verifying the ancient saying, "when the student is ready, the teacher will appear."

Predictably, the direct teacher student time ends. The teacher moves on, and the student is left to integrate, practice and perfect what he has learned. The most significant of which universally appears to be compassion, faith, and love.

Ultimately, the day comes when the hero must return from whence he came; not to boast of his accomplishments, or to gloat that he was right to dream and believe, but out of love and compassion for those fledgling souls, like he once was, with that intense yearning to do, to learn, to have, to become; who sense in their spirits, what he now knows in spirit and in truth – seagulls really can fly.

Bibliography

Coogan, Michael D., ed. *Eastern Religions.* New York: Oxford University Press, 2005.

Fluker, Walter, *They Looked for a City.* Lanham: University Press, 1989.

Lincoln, C. Eric, ed. *Martin Luther King, Jr.: A Profile.* Farrar, Strauss, and Giroux, 1985.

Nolan, Timothy, Leonard D. Goodstein, and William Pfeiffer, *Plan or Die 101 Keys to Organizational Success.* Pfeiffer, 1993.

Templeton, John, *Wisdom from World Religions: Pathways toward Heaven on Earth.* Radon: Temple Foundation Press, 2002.

Williams, Juan, *This Far by Faith.* New York: Harper Collins, 2003

www.ingramcontent.com/pod-product-compliance
Lightning Source LLC
LaVergne TN
LVHW010549100826
845148LV00013B/2675

* 9 7 9 8 2 1 8 8 7 4 1 7 9 *